bahrisons

bahrisons
chronicle of a bookshop

Anuj Bahri with Debbie Smith
from the narrations of Balraj Bahri

Swankit
a division of India Research Press

All rights reserved by publisher. No part of this publication,
may be reproduced, stored in or introduced into a retrieval system
or transmitted in any form, or by any means, electronic, mechanical,
photocopying, recording or otherwise without the prior written
permission of the publisher of this book..

Designed by anuj bahri.
cover credit – Rajni M.

2004 © India Research Press, New Delhi.

ISBN : 81-87943-46-7

**bahrisons...chronicle of a bookshop
from the narrations of Balraj Malhotra**

Cataloguing in Publication Data

ISBN : 81-87943-46-7

Bahrisons...chronicle of a bookshop
1. Partition.   2. Biography. 3. Indian. 4. Title.

Printed in India at Focus Impressions, New Delhi – 110 003.

created by
India Research Press
B-4/22, Safdarjung Enclave, New Delhi – 110 029.
Ph.: 24694610; Fax : 24618637
www.indiaresearchpress.com
contact@indiaresearchpress.com ; bahrisons@vsnl.com

The Malhotra family at their home in Ritz Lines, Delhi.

Acknowledgements

With my 75th birthday approaching this year and, more importantly, the 50th anniversary of the shop, my son Anuj thought that it would be a nice memento to publish a chronicle of my bookshop and my life based on my reminisces. This was something of a last-minute idea and it is hard work under pressure that has brought the book to publication. For this I would like thank Anuj, Debbie Smith and Ravi.

I would also like to thank K.B.S. Chopra, Vishwa Vij, D.K. Berry and Subodh Kaura for their advice and interest in the project and all those who took the time from busy lives to write in with felicitations and stories of a relationship that has spanned many years.

Thanks to my able staff, in the present and over the past 50 years. And, of course, my family - for sharing their memories and for their support.

Foreword

I first met Balraj Bahri (or Bahri Saheb as he is popularly called) in the mid-seventies, when I was a young management trainee with Macmillan. I must add that I was quite terrified, for making a sales trip to Bahri Sons in those days was considered a nightmare by most salesmen. Yet even though Bahri Saheb was famous for his quick temper he was respected and courted by salesmen because he was also known to order generous quantities of titles he fancied.

So, there I was, quaking in my boots at the prospect of coming face to face with a tall, handsome, though tough-looking, man with an impressive moustache. Predictably, like everyone else, I was asked to leave because Bahri Saheb never met any salesmen after lunch.

This happened several times, but I was determined that I must meet him only after lunch, for I knew that no salesman ever dared to visit Bahri Sons between one and seven in the afternoon. And that, I thought, gave me perfect opportunity to get Bahri Saheb's undivided attention. So I persisted with my calls.

Then, one day, I found Bahri Saheb in a good mood. As I came into the shop, he asked me what I was carrying inside my bag. I don't know if he liked the samples I showed him but from the way he asked me in, I knew I had struck a chord with a fellow book lover. Ever since then, I made it a habit to see Bahri Saheb only after lunch: not only did I get his undivided attention I got a good cup of tea in the bargain.

Later, when I started Roli Books, his advice on what kind of titles to publish, his views on pricing and authors helped me considerably. This confirmed what I had always known: that behind his tough exterior and bristling moustache, Mr. Bahri is a genuine, honest and a very frank person. He has helped me immeasurably in developing a good instinct for books.

Alas, these days my trips to his shop as salesman

are rare. I still wish I could visit him after lunch carrying a salesman's black bag. For in my heart I know that even if I get no orders, I will come back with bags full of wisdom.

Pramod Kapoor
Roli Books

Preface

This is the story of my father who has carved out a unique niche in the world of books. His story began in a small village in what is now Pakistan, which he left at the age of nineteen. Memories linger and this is a journey through his life, through the historically rich flavours of the past; the happy days of childhood, the ups and downs of day-to-day living, the fight for survival and the turns of fate that lead to fulfillment in unexpected ways. Today he is a well known figure in the literary world, is looked up to and is role model for his family and friends. When you meet this man, he is just like you or me, but the flame in his eyes...the burning desire to survive and achieve, that is what separates him from the ordinary. I have known him all my life, but really met him for the first time today.

The second born in a family of four children, Balraj was oblivious to the worries of life in his teenage years, when his main goal was to be a good son and a bright student. Aims were high but achievements low, a result of circumstance, and the need was always to do better. Then came the disastrous tragedy that separated the east from the west and his home town was not his any longer. Just one day in history and he was nothing more than another refugee among the millions that fled Pakistan looking for safety. Awake for endless nights, he was on the hunt for a future, for shelter and a safe passage for his family.

Landed in a strange city, along with his elder brother Devinder, he found himself hawking railway carriage seats for a living...or, loading and unloading a bullock-drawn carriage at the railway station. At that time...what else could he do? The young ones and elderly had to be cared for - he had mouths to feed - and always he had to be prepared for the challenges the next sunrise would bring.

1

Not so long ago, I remember entering a little bookshop in a busy market in Lutyens' Delhi. The shop was right in the centre of the market and business was in progress; telephones rang, books were being paid for, customers were browsing and asking for assistance. There was bustle and movement and there he was, seated in one corner in the midst of all this activity, going through the catalogues, his daily ritual, selecting the books to order for his customers.

"Keeping yourself up-to-date is the key to being able to help your readers, " was what he always said.

I watched him. Immersed in his reading he still managed to keep an eye on his customers and to take note of what each one needed. I waited a while longer, browsing along with the others, and then moved closer to where he was seated. With sharp eyes and graying hair, he had an air of confidence and looked the master of his surroundings. From time to time, he would look up to make sure that all was well and return to his reading with a small smile of satisfaction.

I approached him with my hand extended, "Hello Sir…." I said and introduced myself. "I am the son of an old customer of yours. I have been living in America and have just returned after twenty years. I wanted to see how our favourite bookseller was doing….!!"

He smiled gently and got up slowly, looking directly at me "Are you not …Mr. Jha's son?" I was amazed that he remembered my family; what my father did, my mother, sisters, even my uncles. He seemed genuinely pleased to see me, just as if he had adopted the role of a father. He seemed to want to help me catch up on the twenty years gone by.

He remembered my father's tastes in reading and how I would visit the shop as a child and sit there, hour after hour, pouring over books I could not afford to buy.

I slowly took his hand in both of mine and he patted the bundle with his free hand.

"Come, sit with me for a while – tell me how your father is...."

Life for him had not changed much. He was always at his bookstore, day after day, year after year, happy watching the young and the old satisfy their hunger for knowledge, browsing through the shelves, stocked with such thought and care, in his little bookshop that he called BAHRI. The name is as familiar to book lovers as the warmth of a fireside after a long cold journey.

"Books are like food, they satisfy your hunger for knowledge and the bookshop is like a good restaurant".... he said. 'The décor, the seating, the ambience and the service are all important when we go out to dine but most important of all is the chef's ability to maintain the quality of the food that you are served. This is what brings you back again and again. And so it is with books – display, presentation and service are essential but most important is a personal knowledge of each customer and the ability to provide the books that meet his needs. It is a difficult profession' he continued 'and progress can be slow – the climb takes many years of dedicated service. Our advertising is word of mouth!'

I have seen such dedication and sincerity at Bahri's bookstore.

.....in my past

2

I will never forget the day when we were forced to abandon our homes and possessions and flee from the land of our birth and forefathers leaving behind all that was part of our very being. In an instant, gone were the smiles and laughter and the love shared with those of different religions on the streets that we knew as home. Shouting and the screams of yet another dying soul filled the air. The days were for the hunters pursuing their victims and the nights heard the grief and terror of the lost and bereaved - those never to be re-united with their loved ones. Numb at heart, yet alive to survival, we moved from house to house, street to street, village to village in our hunt for safety.

Within twenty-four hours the fate of millions had altered and there was no way back. Friends, those we thought of as brothers, life long neighbours refused to look us in the eyes and ask us to stay and live together as we had always done.

I was not a bookseller then, just a young man of nineteen who had thoughts of doing something a little different with my life, if only in a small way. I wanted to try something other than working the land or going into service, the traditional occupations of my family in the past. An engineer perhaps or a school teacher, but the owner of a successful bookshop in an alien city – not in my wildest dreams.

I was the second born in a family of four children, uncles, aunts and cousins; a happy and loving network of extended family that would be a great boon to me in later years. We, the Malhotras, were upper caste Hindu Kshatriya Punjabis and Malakwal (now in Pakistan) was our home. My mother was strong, pious and hard working. My good natured and easygoing father was the respected manager of the only Bank in the busy wholesale market and railway junction town of Mandi

Bha-u-ddin

Life was simple then. Hindus, Muslims – what was the difference? We lived as one; brothers of the same street. Agitation and uprisings, when they happened, were not communal. The two communities were united and fought against a common enemy, the foreigners in our homeland. But to fight each other was unheard of. Yet on that day we could hear cries from across the boundary of our house, cries of friends begging for their lives to be spared. In my younger days I had heard tales of demons who set foot on earth to rid it of the human race and human decency. It seemed as though those demons were amongst us again stamping out all that was good.

My brothers and sisters and I shared an ordinary childhood much like that of all the other children of the area, centred on our school life. There were no cars or buses and a long walk brought us to the sanctity of education. We were never given any money to spend en-route. Though difficult, learning was fun in those days; the teachers were dedicated to their profession and devoted to their students.

My older brother Devinder and I were always close, did a lot together and shared many moods together. But there was one occasion that bought spice and sparkle into our young minds and which instilled a life long passion in me. The very anticipation of this forbidden event added excitement to the routine of our lives.

The *zamindars* or landowners would organise a *Mujra** in a neighbouring village and invite a select group of their friends to attend. A tradition very much enjoyed in the Punjab, the *mujra* was not classical dance and music but what came to be called 'nautch' by the British. When a *mujra* was announced, a group of about fifteen to twenty men would gather at the host *zamindar's* house to enjoy the entertainment. There were no cars; the affluent would travel by horse, the rest by bicycle or on foot.

Our father's youngest brother lived in the village of Kadaranbad, now in Pakistan. With no formal education, this uncle liked to stay in the fields all day.

---

* A performance by singing and dancing girls for a male audience

He enjoyed looking after his land, a vast acreage given to our forefathers as a gift by the British Government in appreciation of their loyalty to the Crown. That made my Uncle the local *zamindar*; a man of taste, wealth and appreciation for all things beautiful, including, of course, the *mujra*.

Devinder and I looked forward to spending time at the family *haveli**. Once there, we begged and pleaded with our Uncle to take us along with him to the *Mujra*. "*Cha Cha***, will you take us also?" and he would say "No" and then reluctantly relent. The *Mujra* was synonymous with prostitution hence his unwillingness to take such young boys with him.

Our enjoyment was heightened by the secrecy with which we had to plan these events. For weeks we would anticipate our next visit to Uncle's *haveli* and, by keeping our ears to the grapevine, we tried to make sure that it coincided with a *mujra*. Then we gave ourselves up to fantasizing about the forbidden pleasures of the

---

* A joint family ancestral home
** Uncle

evening; who would the performer be? What would she look like? Would she dance more or sing more? And, above all, what would she wear?

Once Uncle relented, we dressed in our finest and followed him on foot while he rode the family horse. He was not just an ordinary person from the village, he was the *zamindar* and he would travel to the celebrations on horseback.

Once we arrived at the venue of the performance, we would begin to relax. Safe in the privacy of the hall with our Uncle's host and his guests, no one took any notice of two young boys as we tried to go unnoticed among the men seated on the floor. The performance was mesmerising. Along with all the men present, we admired the courtesan; the way she walked, sang, danced and the skill with which she tantalised and had us frozen to our seats. Money, thrown in appreciation of her style, would be lying thick on the floor around her as she danced and sang. The hall rang with sounds of appreciation and the calls, sometimes obscene, of the men inviting the dancer over to their corner of the room. The winner was the man with the deepest pockets.

Wo husn ki ada
wo pajeb ki jhankaar
wo khule kambron ki band roshni....!!

Yaad hain mujhe kuch dhundle se lamhe
Wo table ki dhaap, wo gazlon ke mukhde....!!

    Mujra generally went on through the night until the early hours of the morning but despite our eagerness to attend these clandestine gatherings we never managed to stay awake and would fall asleep after a few dances. But I still carry with me a love of this tradition and of *qawali** which I also attended as a young lad. Today I seek out and appreciate *qawali* although the dying tradition of *mujra* is now only practiced for the very rich or in far away places like Lucknow. Elsewhere it has degenerated beyond recognition.

• • •

    With the passing of childhood came the question

---

*   *Qawali* is the singing of Urdu couplets set to music. Though devotional in origin, based on the sayings of Sufi mystics, it is also performed for popular entertainment. Qawali and mujra were never scheduled together; women danced and sang at the mujra while men usually performed the devotional qawali.

of higher education. The cut off class was the 10th, or Matriculation as it was known in those days and higher education was limited to a privileged few, either due to economic circumstances or family tradition. Students with an aptitude for learning who received high marks had the chance to progress to college or the 14th as it was called and to University.

In the past, a few of my relatives went into service - my great-grandfather had been in the police - but the family were traditionally landowners and enjoyed working the land. My grandfather had been offered the post of forest officer by the British but turned it down, preferring to remain a landlord. It was my father's generation who began to move away from the family home and traditional occupation into service. At that time, only my Uncle carried on the family custom of working the land.

Money was not plentiful in my family. Father earned a modest salary from his work at the bank and Devinder, as soon as he had completed his 10th, followed our father into service with the bank to help support the family. I then had the luxury of being able to join University, a rare occurrence in my family, and I thank my older brother for this opportunity as his contribution to the family income gave me the freedom to pursue further education.

The transition from school to college was not difficult for me in spite of the fact that the college in Rawalpindi was huge, with students and educationists from all over India. It was in that environment that my dedication to learning grew and the desire to achieve something more than was expected of me by tradition.

3

My college years were also the years when the uprising for freedom had reached its peak. Leaders from all over the nation gathered and held rallies and programs. Events were organized to cultivate a feeling of nationalism in the hearts of the young. The nation was together as one, in union, demanding the right to freedom from the Crown. The British were naturally opposed to such activities and made every effort to ensure they did not succeed. They managed to subdue many of these events but the desire for freedom continued to grow in people's hearts.

The British had effectively used their policy of divide and rule for centuries and once more it came into effect, with truly tragic results. In the past this strategy had been aimed at the rulers of the princely states – Rajasthan, the Punjab, the Deccan - but now it was applied to the highest authorities ruling the nation; the statesmen and leaders that the vast population listened to and looked up to.

The freedom movement, exemplary in its dedication and selflessness, was betrayed by the emergence of the greedy and corrupt politician who having newly tasted power was willing to sacrifice all for his own immediate gain. The masses were illiterate and these politicians, in their selfish love for power and its rewards, swayed the emotions of the simple people from love and brotherhood to hatred for one another. These political instigators used all their wiles and venom to corrupt the masses by using the one issue before which most of mankind has found itself helpless – that of religion. This mass hatred was achieved by influencing the religious leaders, the Mullahs and Pundits, who had the power to sway the minds of the people.

Thus the seeds of hatred and the demand for

separate nations were sown in the minds of the common man. The religious divide that separated the Hindu population from the non-Hindus was created. Shockingly, the friend with whom one had lived peaceably all ones life was now the enemy ready to do one great harm.

Relationships were broken and finally came the tragic Partition and the nation was involved in the biggest bloodbath the world ever witnessed.

4

Atrocity mounted on atrocity. Homes were burnt, human beings slaughtered. Entire families were wiped out. Relatives running a few paces behind their kin were lost forever. Husbands were separated from their families, wives raped and killed and children, screaming, ran from person to person searching for their parents.

Sometimes it would begin from one end of the *mohulla**; a sound like a whisper, coming nearer, becoming louder until realisation dawned that a crowd of maddened people, screaming and abusing, had

---

* Ward

become a walking ball of fire, burning all that came in its path. Today it would be Muslims, tomorrow Hindus; the houses to the right tonight, in another place tomorrow. They were out to kill and out for revenge. It was truly a kind of madness; they did not know what they were doing or why but the power to convince had been so well used on them that their minds were filled with hatred for their brothers.

The streets were full of the blood of Hindus and Muslims. What was the difference? Until now they had been one. Attempt at a normal life was out the question. Schools were closed, offices broken into, fires smoldered in ruined buildings.

Daylight brought teams of rescue workers who took care of the dead and dying. Night bought silence and terror. Families would seek sanctuary in one house then another, looking for places to hide. With dawn came relief and gratitude that they had survived another night but also the heartbreaking search for loved ones.

My family was part of the Hindu *mohulla*. In the towns Hindus were usually the majority, Malakwal had about 500 Hindu families, but in the countryside and small villages around us, Muslims dominated. In those days the Hindus were the educated class and were businessmen or office workers. The Muslims tended towards manual labour; in the fields and factories: as carpenters, plumbers and masons.

Until this parting we had existed together, Hindu and Muslim, sharing resources from the local well to the school and, when the need arose, even the same house. The two communities knew everything about one each other's households, work, lives. Perhaps that is why the destruction was so devastating; we knew so much of one another.

Even before August 15, the Independence Day of India and Pakistan, we had moved from our ancestral home. Then came the rioting and destruction and we took refuge for a few days in the local Police Station.

At this time a large Cotton Factory had been set up as a temporary camp for the fleeing Hindus. Hindus of one area would gather at one location and try to form a larger group and then move on to the next location and so on until each night a sizeable group would make their way to the Cotton Factory where they would be given food and shelter.

After two days, we were transferred from the Police Station to the Cotton Mill where rations had been arranged from what was left, after looting and burning, in the Hindu shops and godowns. Volunteers, along with the police, provided security and guidance to newcomers and every help was given in the search for lost relatives.

We remained in the camp for about ten days, waiting and hoping along with all the others, to be transported by some means to India. Amritsar was the first stop on the Indian side across the newly created border and this is where we were most likely to be taken. We waited eagerly for the longed for day of departure to India unaware that it would bring with it the worst crises we had yet endured.

5

The day of departure finally arrived and we left the security of the Cotton Mill. We were heavy with sorrow at what we must leave behind but at the same time desperate to go, not wanting to spend another terror filled night in Malakwal.

We arrived at Malakwal station, along with crowds of fellow refugees, my father and mother, younger brother and sister. Devinder was still employed at his bank in Rawalpindi and was not able to join us. Alone, he would try to make the journey across to India as soon as he was able. We had lost contact with the rest of our relatives at Kadaranbad and had no means of knowing if they had survived.

There was chaos at Malakwal Station. People and more people, hundreds and thousands, swarmed onto the platform, their eyes straining up the track for a sight of the train and the chance to be the first to board. Like all the other souls desperate to get away, we hoped to squeeze ourselves onto the severely overcrowded train. Determined, my father and I at last succeeded in making our way into an already overcrowded third class compartment. Under normal circumstances the conditions would have been unbearable but we felt relieved and grateful that we had made it. But fear would not abate until we reached the safety of Amritsar and maybe not even then. My mother and sister wept, through sorrow for what was lost and from the fearful anxiety of what we were living through. With Devinder away, I now had the duty of being the eldest son and the weight of responsibility that went with it. My younger brother was just a little boy needing our love and protection.

Hour after painful hour passed while we waited for the train to move, stuffed into the carriages but not daring to move. We were able to bear anything as long as we kept our hard won places on the train. When the train gave a sudden jerk and began at last to pull out of the station there were screams of joy.

We were to travel to Amritsar and to safety. But how could we be sure? Until a very short time ago Amritsar had been part of the same country - our country - and now it was in another nation divided from us by a border. But it was our best chance.

We traveled on for about an hour and pulled into the main junction town of Mandi Bha-ud-din. Passengers stood up, puzzled, but there were more people to pick up and squeeze on to the already overcrowded train. As soon as the train stopped at the platform another mass of humanity surged forward and pushed to board. Finally there was no more room for even a small child and then came the quiet of waiting which grew to a strained silence and mounting tension. The train had halted for much longer than was expected.

Then it happened. There was movement and whispering at the door of our boogie. Some official looking men, Muslims, had boarded the train. The whispers became audible, passengers were telling the newcomers that the man they were looking for was not on board. I was gripped by dread when I saw the expression on my father's face. He recognised the men, knew where they were from and my terror increased when I heard these men shout out my father's name.

My father was pulled off the train and we all followed him, not wanting to be separated from him for even an instant. My father stood on the platform with his family gathered close to him. We had begun to realise through our paralysing fear that these men were co-workers from our father's bank. They had come to take him off the train because they needed him - his expertise. In that entire region they had not been able find someone to replace my father and they wanted him to continue to run the bank and to keep it open. My mother, younger brother and sister screamed and protested, begging for our father to be allowed to leave with us or failing that, for us to be permitted to stay with him in Pakistan. We only knew that we did not want to be separated from him. We had no confidence that he would be safe and preferred a future in which we all stayed together whatever the dangers.

Then one man stepped forward from the others, a

man whom I had known all my life, whose son was my childhood friend. Addressing my mother, he pulled this son from the crowd and, putting his hand on the boy's head, swore he would take responsibility for her husband's safe return. He explained that the bank needed him during this transition period to help train new staff. He would be allowed to leave after six months. If the family wished to stay they would do their best to take care of us but it was too risky and he strongly advised my mother to re-board the train with her children and to continue the journey to safety

My father agreed to stay, saying that if it was his destiny he would be re-united his family after a few months. The train had already been considerably delayed by this incident and reluctantly, dazedly, my mother and the three of us re-boarded.

As the train chugged relentlessly towards India we were being distanced from all the horrors we had witnessed but also from our father, brother, relatives and the land of our birth. We were being carried forward to a new, uncertain future but could not think of that now. As we drew closer to Amritsar our new status began to dawn on us. We were refugees.

6

Shattered, we reached Amritsar!

    We did not know anyone in this city. We were separated from all our relatives and had nowhere to go. Like vagabonds, we disembarked and stood on the platform. The train had brought us to an unknown world and this new life without elders, without our father and with the immense responsibility of the young ones to look after, weighed heavily on me. Tentatively we moved away from the station with the crowds of refugees, just like us, who carried only a bag full of clothing and uncertainty of what their futures would hold.

    We did not know a soul but thought my mother's

younger brother, who was an inspector in the police, may have been posted in the Amritsar area on emergency duty. We prayed that we would find him somehow but without an address we did not have much hope. At that moment we had more immediate concerns. We only had a little money and by the end of the day we had to have a roof over our heads and safe lodgings. My mother and I and the two young ones walked aimlessly in search of shelter and food.

A camp similar to the one at Malakwal had been arranged at Amritsar. Following a group of refugees and with the guidance of local volunteers, we reached the camp. I could hear fervent discussions all around me about who had been left behind and who had made it across the border. I was rarely a part of these discussions. I have always approached life with optimism and did not have the patience to play back the past. I was eager to create new ground and directions to follow. Now, in my older years I enjoy looking back!

I could not be certain that my father would ever come back. I tried to have faith in the oath of my friend's father, the oath he had taken on his son's life guaranteeing the safe return of my father. But the hatred I had witnessed when we were uprooted and thrown out of our home made me fear greatly for my father's safety, despite this promise. Unsure, my mother and I had to wait and hope that tomorrow, if not today, my father would send a message...but how would he find us?

A day after our arrival in Amritsar I wrote a letter to my father and addressed it to the bank, another to Devinder and yet another to the rest of the family left behind in our native village, to let them know that Amritsar was our base. It felt like shooting arrows in the dark; I doubted the letters would be delivered but had to try something. My mother rarely asked questions or said much about her feelings but her eyes showed her doubts and worries, longing and fear. But when she looked at her sons they held trust and confidence. She knew her questions could not be answered yet and that she would have to endure the agony of waiting. I was always close to my mother and I think it eased her to have me there. I was able to question the volunteers and fellow refugees for advice and on the options open to us.

After a couple of weeks we settled into the routine of camp life, managing to get enough food and clothing to sustain our bodies but our minds needed to know more. I joined a small group of boys and went out every morning to roam the streets in search of work ...any work.... that would keep me busy and provide an income to support my family. But work was difficult to find. I was unknown in this part of the country, one of thousands, a refugee to be pitied but not necessarily enough to be offered a job!

There was curiosity; people wanted to know how many members of the family we had left behind, how many had been killed, what had become of homes and property, what compensation the government would provide, what our plans for the future were and so on, but no one wanted the liability of providing us with shelter or to share work with us. Most of the jobs we - the other boys and I - managed to find were on the roadside or in shops; low paying menial jobs. I was not swayed from my goal. My mother and I had a guiding motive - to be reunited with my father. We would remain in Amritsar for as a long as it took to hear from him. Only then would we think of moving on to better prospects.

On one of the many days when I was roaming the streets with my group of friends in search of work, I saw a familiar face. I had an inkling it was someone known to my family and then there was the thrill of recognition. By complete chance I had come upon the uncle who was posted in Amritsar. Uncle recognised me immediately and hugged me. Now there was hope. He put me in his jeep and drove straight to the camp to be re-united with his sister and her other children. It was good to see smiles and laughter and the relief in my mother's eyes.

We packed quickly and were ready to move. Uncle gathered us all together and drove us to his home, a large bungalow with many rooms. Big hearted, he opened the doors of his house to his sister and her children for as long as we wished to stay. We lived with him for over a month.

Then a letter arrived from my father. He was well

and hoped to join us in a few months. The day finally came when he and Devinder crossed the border and the family were together again at last.

7

News began to arrive of other members of the family - aunts, uncles and cousins - who had moved across to India and were settling into camps in and around Delhi. My father and Uncle decided that we should move on to Delhi to try and find the rest of our scattered relatives. Once re-united, we would decide collectively on what course of action to follow. Furthermore, my Uncle told us of the various schemes the Government had introduced for refugees; we learned that we may be eligible to land grants in lieu of the property we had been forced to leave behind in our native village. My father and Devinder could apply for jobs in a bank as compensation for the ones that had been taken away in what had now become Pakistan. With the hope of receiving some compensation with which to make a fresh start we decided to move to Delhi.

Within a few months of arriving in Amritsar we were packed once again - nomads by circumstance but in search of a more settled life – and we boarded the train bound for Delhi.

I have always liked to sit at the window on a moving train watching the countryside, villages and people flash by - catching glimpses into other lives. Traveling on unending miles of track we carry with us our hopes and memories and our attachment to people and places. Thousands of dreams travel in the carriages on every single journey. The train will continue on to other destinations but it is pre-determined where we leave the track. I sat alone on my berth, looking forward to the end of this tiring journey and wondering what it would bring.

Delhi – a city of dreams – was approaching, coming closer and closer with every passing town. I had no idea what awaited me but I was looking forward to my new life.

8

It was early morning. Slowly the train drew into the platform. I stood at the door watching crowds of people moving about busy in their purpose. Vendors of tea, newspapers and those with tiny kiosks displaying their wares were cleaning and sweeping the small area around their shops. The homeless were all around, some alone, some with families, all watching the arrival of yet more refugees.

We had now mastered the art of reaching a new and unknown place and within hours making it our home. To survive was a skill that I had learned on this journey and on the streets. This was not just another city but the city we hoped would be our final destination and our home. Keeping close to each other, we were relieved to leave the confines of the overcrowded boogie and breathe the crisp air of a Delhi morning. It was freezing cold and the fog had not lifted yet. Cooking fires were being lit all around and the thick smoke wafted upwards giving the reassuring feel of the start of another normal day. Young children sleeping on the platform huddled together for warmth under a single quilt while their mothers were busy completing the rituals of their morning chores, blind to the crowds walking across the little patch of platform that was their temporary home.

The exit was only a few steps away and we began to move across the platform towards it. As I walked forward I felt mounting anticipation tinged with apprehension for, once I left the confines of the station, Iwould have to face this new and unknown world. But the hardship of the past few months had ignited a fire in me so that, though afraid and unsure, I now had the courage to face the challenges that came my way. The journey was long and we were tired, yet our aim was to be united and to look for a suitable place to camp.

This time we had the address of a camp where our relatives were staying and just enough money provided by our Uncle for the expense of the journey. My mother had quietly and practically saved much of this for a greater need. Our immediate concern was to find this camp without wasting any more of our meagre savings. An iron trunk on our heads and shoulders hurting with the weight, Devinder and I walked towards a new life.

We made our way to the camp set up by the Delhi government for refugees. It was the largest temporary settlement ever to have been constructed. We stood on the dusty track leading to the camp commandant's tent – four children and our mother with two trunks and two gunny sacks - while our father went to have us registered at Kingsway Camp!

9

Being registered as a refugee was not difficult. The officials had gone through the formalities thousands of times and the procedure took just fifteen minutes. We were entered on the daily register of the camp and assigned a barrack not far from the main camp office. Courteous volunteers helped us to our quarters and it was a relief to feel secure at last and to have somewhere to stay and set up home. The first thing my mother did on entering her new domain was to sit down to pray and to thank God for the mercy he had shown by bringing the family through safely.

We were exhausted from the wearying, anxiety filled months that we had lived through and that night we all slept deeply, oblivious to the sounds of the camp around us.

The next morning my parents set out to look for the relatives they had been told were at Kingsway camp. We, the children, took the morning to recover slowly, to laze about and discover our new surroundings. We lay side by side discussing the difficult days we had just passed through. It was good that we were all together. The bond between Devinder and me grew stronger. We thought alike.

Our parents' search was successful and they returned to our barracks with Uncle Ram Lal and a few of my mother's Aunts. After so many months of hardship we at last experienced joy and the pleasure of seeing our parents laugh and smile and chat. After hours of talk and discussion, we all sat down - parents, children, aunts and uncles - to share a simple meal. *Roti** and onions was all we could spare but we enjoyed it like a feast. Perhaps it was on this first day that I began to turn away from the past and the months of mourning and look, with optimism and hope, towards the future.

---

* Type of bread

10

The morning sunlight broke into our barracks through the glass windows on the eastern side, illuminating the room with a fresh golden glow. My mother was always the first to rise and would begin her day with *puja**, giving her thanks to God and chanting as she went about her morning chores. She was sweeping the floor around us when I awoke. I stood watching the sunrise over the trees I could see through the window. My mother came and stood with me and I put my arm reassuringly on her shoulder. I was very close to my mother and these past months had brought us even closer. Watching a new morning unfold I think we both wondered what

---

* Prayer

the next step would be. The urgent priority was to earn a living.

It took me a few days to familiarise myself with the camp - its communal latrines and communal kitchen. Our relatives, particularly my young cousins who had already been at the camp a few months, showed us around and helped us get organised. The authorities supplied basic rations to the camp and the refugees would use the communal kitchen to cook their own food. The women took care of household chores and cooking. Devinder and I must now think of finding work.

Once again our cousins helped. Chatting with them at night we learned of the long fruitless hours spent searching for work - any work - and that the only odd jobs that came their way were menial: errand boys or shop workers. It was then that an enterprising group of young cousins and their friends told us that they had discovered a way of making eight to ten rupees a day each, a handsome sum in those days. They were happy to let us join their group.

Used to months of hardship and scrimping and

saving, this amount seemed improbable to us brothers but we were overjoyed at the chance of employment. As agreed the night before, we made our way to the Railway Station where we joined the rest of the group for the usual breakfast of *chai* and *paranthas**.

The railway station was already bursting with life and movement and Devinder and I followed the rest of the group. One or two members remained on the platform but the rest of us made our way to the open sheds where the trains were parked overnight for their routine maintenance. We boarded the empty carriages, two or three boys per compartment, and stretched ourselves out on the seats and waited. Eventually the train pulled out of the sheds towards the platform to pick up its passengers.

The boys who had been left on the platform had been busy. In those days, second class seats on the train could not be reserved and were sold on a first come first serve basis. Once the train reached the platform it was a free for all.

---

* Type of fried bread

It was the job of the boys on the platform, the negotiators', to offer the seats that we had been keeping warm on the journey from shed to station to desperate passengers for the huge sum of Rs. 5! These seats would then be released to these fee-paying customers.

Devinder and I were able to take home, on our first day, the unthinkable sum of Rs. 16!

11

Sixteen rupees was a large amount of money in those days and we could not believe our good fortune. We were overjoyed with what we had managed to earn for so little effort. In spite of the free bus ride (provided by the Government) from the city to the camp, the two of us wanted to walk home. It was exciting and encouraging to have earned so much money in just one day and we wanted to prolong the anticipation of the moment when we handed over our earnings to my mother. We ran the few remaining yards to our barracks.

That night there was a small celebration. In the community kitchen, our mother happily prepared, besides the daily ration of *dal** and *roti,* a plateful of vegetables. Her sons had brought home their first earnings and we would dine in style.

So began a new routine centred on earning a living. The entire day would be spent out and about, first at the station pursuing our unusual and - if I may add - enterprising scheme that guaranteed an income and then on the lookout for other forms of work. Devinder and I were close but now a deeper understanding had grown between us. We both knew that the job at the station was a temporary stepping stone to more steady work.

True to the hard working character of the Punjabi, the more we worked the happier we were. This had less to do with a desire for wealth or status as an inability to remain idle and a need to work for works sake. So, although we managed to earn a living at the station we were always on the lookout for new opportunities.

Devinder and I now had a network of friends and

---

*   Lentils

contacts and through them we discovered that the city administration were offering licences for the operation of rickshaws. We applied at once and were granted two licences. But what were we to do for rickshaws? We used our station earnings to commission two custom-made rickshaws and then hired these out on a daily basis at Rs 10 per day. We had opened our first business. There was not much work involved, our father kept an eye on the enterprise, and we were free to keep looking.

Months passed in this way. Many more of our relatives had been traced. Our Uncle - of whom Devinder and I had fond memories, the very Uncle who had smuggled us into the *Mujra* - and his elder brother had settled in Karnal with their families. Two more of my father's brothers were located at a different camp in Delhi.

We were now settled in the camp but it still felt temporary to me. A few more years would pass before I began to think of the camp as home.

My mother meanwhile made the best of this new life and created a home for us. She had a large circle of friends and they would spend the afternoons together once the housework was done. Much of her time was spent praying at the *mandir** that existed at the base of a beautiful old *peepul* tree close to our barracks. Others would gather there at fixed times in the day and the evening for prayer sessions. The air would ring with the melody of the chants and the playing of the *dholak* ** accompanied by the jangle of the *manjeeras*. The first idol of Lord Rama was soon placed there and the makeshift prayer ground grew into Ram Mandir.

Devinder had always been interested in politics and he volunteered with the National Congress and attached himself in service to the local MLA.

Devinder and I continued to keep our eyes and ears open for new opportunities. We learned that the Government of India Publications Department at Metcalf House had put out a tender for the loading and unloading of Government publications from the Railway Station to the warehouses and vice versa. Very

---

* Temple
* A percussion instrument

Young Balraj in the year 1955.

Balraj's parents and sister at Ritz Lines, Delhi.

Balraj's grandmother 1957.

Balraj's mother at thebirth of the first grandchild.

Devinder 'Netaji' with political group sharing a moment with (late) Prime Minister Smt. Indira Gandhi. (Left Corner)

Devinder getting ready for a scooter excurtion with friends. (Right Corner)

Patriotic Devinder saluting the Indian Flag on Independence day. (Right Corner)

Young Saubhagya year 1955.

Swaran Lata at home.

Balraj and Saubhagya at their wedding ceremony and the day after.

Saubhagya with her elder sister and nephews.

Saubhagya with friends at office.

Swaran Lata, Saubhagya and Balraj at a family function.

Balraj enjoying a relaxed sunday.

Balraj with friend Peter Hess at home.

Balraj at a picnic with other traders from Khan Market.

Surveying the shops with the local VIP at a regular inspection of Khan Market.

'Brotherhood' - moments with Yassar Arafat.

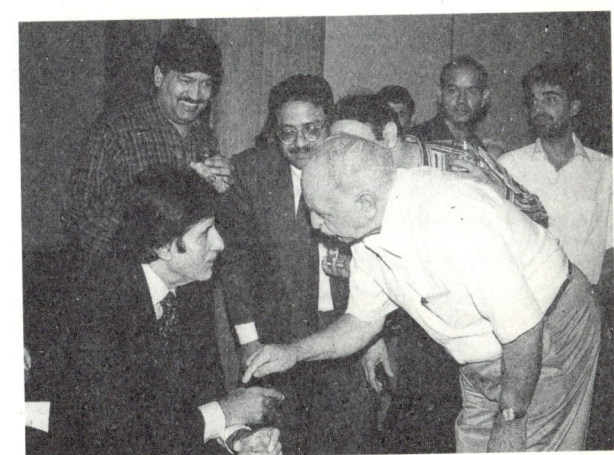

'Words of wisdom' - lighter moments with the the big 'B'.

Introducing the younger generation to the trade....
Balraj and Anuj in discussion.

few bidders applied so my brother and I seized the chance. We secured our bid, hired a bullock cart and driver and were in business yet again. This time, there was a degree of supervision involved but once it was up and running we put our father in charge and this business, too, more or less took care of itself. So what next?

Our contacts at the warehouse gave us information on benefits being offered by the Government to compensate for land, homes and jobs lost in Pakistan. Devinder was eager for a job in a bank similar to the one he had had in Rawalpindi and after many inquiries he was at last rewarded with one.

We had never shirked work. We knew that to survive we had to turn our hands to anything and we performed our duties with willingness and dedication. We had become friends with the staff at the warehouse and our hard work was noticed as was the fact that we were both educated. Our immediate supervisor at the publications division gave us the additional responsibility of getting the goods we transported by bullock cart booked and documented at the station.

Shortly afterwards we heard of another Government tender for an agency for their publications. The officers made an exception and without floating the tender, awarded the agency to us. Thus the first seeds of the Bahri family enterprise were sown.

12

Devinder was the eldest son and the agency was allotted in his name. Devinder continued to work full-time at the bank for some months and would join my father and me at the newly opened shop in the evenings, after work. Our father sat at the shop full time which was opposite the Red Fort and is still run by Devinder and his children today.

I worked at the shop and in my spare time I also volunteered at a social services camp. I was absorbed by the work I did there and found it rewarding. But there was another reason for my dedication to the cause of social services. It was there that I met the two women who were to become part of my future and who would, in their different ways, change my life completely.

Swarn Lata was from Lahore in Pakistan but her family had moved to India before the partition and had managed to retain much of their wealth. Though younger than me she had maturity beyond her years and was calm and serene. Balanced in her thoughts and actions I came to respect her advice and, although at first it was difficult for me, to accept her help. She provided the support and guidance that I had been looking for. She was not afraid to point out my mistakes and was always ready to help. She became a sister to me. Over the years we came to rely on each other's judgment and shared a bond that lasted her lifetime. She passed away nine years ago.

At that time, though, Saubhagya claimed more of my thoughts and was certainly, to me, the more interesting of the two. A close friend of Swarn Lata's, she was beautiful and shy with lovely eyes and I could not keep my eyes off her. Saubhagya too was from a refugee family, from the mysterious rich lands of Dera Ismail Khan. She was destined to become my wife and still stands beside me today.

13

Under the Marina Hotel in Connaught Place - which is still there today - one of my relatives ran a large showroom where he sold imported pens. Shortly after our agency opened in Lajpath Rai Market I began working for this relative as a door to door salesman of pens on a commission basis. The job was full time so while my father ran the agency and my brother worked at the bank, I went to this shop in Connaught Place. In the evening all three of us would meet at our shop and stay there until 8.30 or 9 at night.

Devinder gave up his job at the bank and began running the agency full-time. He put me in touch with a local politician who ran a small shop selling pens at

Chandni Chowk and I was offered a job. Although the shop was not particularly prestigious, the politician was away from the premises much of the time pursuing his political career and left most of the running of his business to me. This was valuable experience and my relationship with the politician also lead to the turning point in my life.

I worked in the this pen shop for about a year and towards the end of this time I began to hear of a market which had been built in New Delhi especially to help the refugees and where shops were being allocated to them.

I was well aware that I had neither the capital to invest nor the experience to undertake such a venture but nevertheless became convinced that this was an avenue worth exploring. But how was I to begin? I turned for advice to Swarn Lata's grandfather who had already opened a shop in Khan Market called Shyam di Hatti which still exists today. He suggested that I ask my employer, the politician, for help. He would have connections and influence and would know the right people to contact.

14

I had some misgivings about approaching my employer. I knew my work was good and that he relied on me and I wondered if he would be willing to let me go. Matters might go the other way and he could use his connections against me! On one of the few occasions when he was actually at the shop I gathered my courage and spoke to him. I pointed out that I had been a sincere and hard worker and that I had been happy working for him and that I knew that he was happy with my work. But I explained that that this was not the end of the line for me. I wanted more. The politician immediately understood that something was expected of him and asked me what I wanted from him. I explained flatly that I wanted a shop of my own and that he was the one who could arrange this for me. The politician pointed out the obvious; that I had no money and only earned Rs. 80 a month working for him. But I insisted that I wanted my own shop. It was with relief that I heard him agree to help and he asked me where I wanted this shop. When I said Khan Market his reaction was 'Oh, the refugee market'.

But he kept his promise and the next day he took me to meet the Minister of Home Affairs who was in charge of Khan Market. I never realised how close he was to the Minister and he introduced me as member of the family and I was welcomed accordingly. He explained to the Minister that 'this boy works for me and he wants a shop in Khan Market'. The Minister agreed at once to allocate a shop to me but explained that there were only a few shops left and that I must go at once to Khan Market and select one. So that is how I came to choose the shop where it is today. It is actually three shops converted to one, part of an original block of four. It was one of the smallest premises in the market and I took it, always aware of the issue of funding.

Then came the first hurdle. In order to secure the

shop premises we had to pay, within a matter of days, the lease of Rs.150 and a security of Rs. 50 or the shop would be given to someone else. But where was I to get this amount? We had no savings and our earnings were used up in day to day living. I went home and discussed this at length with my family and my mother came up with the solution. She sold one of her gold bangles and gave me the money.

Three days later we had the papers of ownership in our hands. The shop had been allotted in Devinder's name as, being the eldest, he was considered head of the family. We were now the proud owners of a shop in an unheard of market far from the familiarity of busy Chandni Chowk, Dariba and Nai Sarak. But the foundation had been laid and the first step taken in creating what was to become Bahrisons.

My new area of operation would be in what was called Lutyen's Delhi or New Delhi, a neighbourhood totally unfamiliar to me. We did not guess at the time that this scheme to benefit refugees, this Khan Market, would one day become such a success.

15

That night there was an air of jubilation in the camp. All my friends and family had gathered at our barracks in a mood to celebrate. In spite of the heavy expenditure we had incurred that morning (and not forgetting how the money had been raised-a secret limited to the immediate family), this evening we were going to enjoy ourselves. To the shop were attached our dreams of a better, more prosperous and secure future. My mother visited the temple to offer thanks and prayers to the Almighty and then returned happily to sit at the kitchen stove - at our request, she had agreed to cook her delicious mutton curry, tandoori roti and *kheer**. We

---

* Rice pudding

were all very happy and the party went on until late at night.

We owned a shop ... but it was empty. When the first burst of pride and satisfaction of ownership had diminished a little we had the most vital questions to answer. What would we sell in our new shop? And how would we pay for the goods and fixtures and fittings?

We might have chosen anything to fill the premises and this made the decision so much harder. I had some experience in selling pens but did not really want to continue on this same path. Now, what to do?

We were in desperate need of advice and once again turned to Swarn Lata's grandfather Shyam. After many long discussions he suggested that as we already had experience in selling stationary and government publications we should try and stay as close to this line as possible. We could always change later if we were not successful. Shyam knew the very man to help us, a member of our extended family network who ran a bookstore in the Connaught Place area quite close to Khan Market. His name was Prem Sagar.

But first we needed fixtures and fittings on which to display our new wares and Shyam put us in touch with his carpenter. The amount quoted for the work was Rs. 500. This was a blow and trying not to be disheartened, on another suggestion from Shyam we went to visit a friend in Sadar Bazar in the Old City. Khanna Stationary Mart was a wholesale dealer for stationary and other products. Here, we found ourselves burdened by the further sum of Rs. 200; the cost of items to start a little stationary counter.

Our enquires had lead to disappointment. Where could we possibly get the unthinkable sum of Rs. 800 when raising a mere Rs. 200 to secure the shop had been such a struggle? We had learnt to take one day at a time, to grasp and make the best of opportunities that came our way and now we experienced doubt. Had we been naïve and over optimistic in buying a shop?

In my life I have had several guardian angels and this time Swarn Lata herself came to my aid. She was close to my family, was trusted and she knew the minimum we had to raise to run just a basic business was Rs. 800. Swarn Lata was aware that we were discouraged and downhearted and offered to lend us the entire amount 'payable when able', as the saying went. Her family was relatively affluent but I was not aware that she had access to funds of her own. Without hesitation she handed over the money we needed. I have never forgotten the extent and depth of this kind gesture.

I could now bounce back to my familiar feeling of optimism. We set about fitting the shop with furniture. We engaged carpenters and bought wood of the best quality (some of it is still in use in the shop today). With this work underway, we went back to Mr. Khanna to order the items we had already short-listed for Rs.200. We looked over the list again, adding some items and deleting others, and ended up with a new account of Rs250. Seeing our enthusiasm and great need to begin work, Mr. Khanna allowed us to take away our revised order and gave us credit of Rs50. We could pay him the next time we came to replenish our stock. A bond developed between us. I saw the elderly Mr. Khanna as a father figure and he in turn treated me like a son. I always remember his trust and kindness that helped us to get started.

We arranged the stationary on our new shelves and felt ready to begin but the shop still looked empty. Our prized goods only filled a few shelves and there was too much vacant unused space.

I remembered Shyam's suggestion to contact Prem Sagar for advice and I went to his shop, Laxshmi Bookstore in Connaught Place, one of the oldest bookshops in Delhi. I had no inkling that this visit would determine the future direction of my life.

Prem Sagar knew my family's story and also knew of my hard work and drive to succeed. That morning he generously shared with me his knowledge of books and running a business and offered me the facilities of his shop. Unbelievably, he gave me credit for the exorbitant sum of Rs. 3500. With a supply of books to the value of this amount we would be able to set up a respectable counter for the sale of books.

Prem Sagar went further. He telephoned other wholesalers and stood guarantee for whatever I needed and even wrote a personal note to W H Smith in London requesting them to open a credit account for me, for which he also stood guarantee. He guided me on the system to follow in my shop.

I was profoundly grateful for all this help but filled with apprehension. I did not know the first thing about the book trade. Having a stock of books was wonderful but I was filled with a sense of panic when I realized that I would have to face the public, my customers and I knew nothing about their tastes and wants and had no knowledge of western titles. How would I know what my customers were asking - it would be impossible to stock every possible title they may request? Then Prem Sagar gave me a simple but vital tip - to keep a pad and pen with me at all times. I could then note down at once a customer's order or any questions he may ask. This was a simple solution to my shortcomings and limited knowledge of the book world-the customer would be my guide.

This was the turning point in my life and I have never forgotten what Prem Sagar did for me and will always be grateful for his generosity, trust and guidance.

So I loaded up a four-seater *'phat-phat'** and set off with my first stock of books to Khan Market. And now at last the shop was open.

---

* A three wheeled motorcycle driven conveyance

Every morning I would get on my bicycle and travel from the camp beyond the Old City and arrive at Khan Market in time to open the shop at 8.30 a.m. sharp. I was never late. Day after day, week after week, I would make notes of my customers' requests. At 1 p.m. I would shut the shop and set off for Connaught Place on my cycle to meet my guide and mentor, Prem Sagar. He would sit with me and go through my precious pad scribbled with the requests of customers. He would then give me the titles I needed from his own shelves. If he did not have them he would send me to the Old City to look for them amongst the stock of other dealers. At 5.30 p.m. I would open the shop again until 8.30 or 9 at night.

As the years passed, I grew in experience and confidence. I began to understand my work and was able to help my customers without always relying on Prem Sagar's kindness. I began to grasp the reading tastes of my clients in the New City and would alter my selection process accordingly. I always tried to put in that extra effort, to go little bit further to meet my customers' demands. I would exhaust every possible source for a book before denying a customer's request.

But it was the people - the customers of this area - who really helped me. Educated and kind, they did not take advantage of my simplicity or ignorance. Encouraged by their patience and forbearance, my knowledge grew.

16

Devinder had been married for some months but I was still a bachelor. Always a hard worker and aware of my duty to my family, I filled my days trying to make the shop a success. I was busy throughout the day, involved with one thing or another, unable to remain idle. My focus was limited to making something of my career and I had only a few personal friends.

Outside work I was carefree and not bound by any restrictions. I have always been fond of the movies, even as a young boy, and would never miss the opportunity to see a film. After a hard day's work I would return home late at night, bathe, have my evening meal and then set off again on my bicycle to the local theatre to see the latest release. Oddly, given the hardship of my early years and at the end of a long work-orientated day I did not go for light entertainment or lose myself in comedy or fantasy. I have always enjoyed movies with a message and realistic themes, even tragedies, and have no interest in *'halla gulla'* or song and dance.

I was desperate to have my feet firmly planted on the ground and my future secure before I made another major move in my life but my fondness for Saubhagya grew with each passing day and I continued to meet her in the afternoons. Her place of work had been shifted to a building near Khan Market and this made it easier for me to call on her during the day. Once again Swaran Lata played a part in my life by bringing me closer to Saubhagya's family of five sisters and their mother.

Saubhagya's family were *zamindars* or owners of ancestral lands from the upper reaches of the Dera Ismail Khan area. Their father had died and they had been left in the care of *Pathans** who risked their own

---

*   Tribe of the North West Frontier region of India and Pakistan.

lives to help the family of women accross the border to safety in India. Our stories were similar; Saubhagya's family had been left with their lives and self respect but all their land and wealth was lost.

Until her daughters were old enough to contribute to the family income, Saubhagya's mother survived by teaching children in the local school. When I met her, Saubhagya worked for the Government in the Department of Rehabilitation. I married her in the year 1955.

17

The shop began to do well and with knowledge of my trade, my confidence grew. I was married and little did I realise the tremendous change this would bring to my life. I now had the added responsibility of a wife and, very soon, of children.

This was a lucky year for us newlyweds. Our first baby, a girl, was born and we named her Neeraj. At work I was now considered a respected member of the traders association, part of the establishment, and was involved with issues on the welfare and progress of the market. With the birth of Neeraj, I took my responsibilities that much more seriously.

In the same year, Saubhagya was allotted

government accommodation not far from the Khan Market area. Throughout I had lived at Kingsway Camp with my parents, brothers and sister and continued to do so after my marriage. With the birth of Neeraj, my wife and I decided to take up the government accommodation and move away from the family. Our new home was much closer to both our places of work which meant we had more leisure time to spend together. So in the year 1958 we left Kingsway Camp to live in New Delhi.

Saubhagya's income sustained the family in the early days of our marriage. Her salary of Rs.120 was more than enough to run a household and provide for a new baby. My wife's contribution also extended to my work. By now, she understood that her husband had dedicated his life to the shop and she adapted her own lifestyle to accommodate my burgeoning career. My work would take me away from the shop from time to time, to make special purchases or establish new suppliers, and Saubhagya would take time off from her own work to manage the shop in my absence.

The shop was established but the profits were

being ploughed back into the business as capital for expansion. The customers' demands for a variety of titles meant that the stock had increased and the shop began to feel cramped. The business was growing and I began to feel the need for larger premises.

I felt I was not contributing enough to the family income to raise the subject of expansion but I discussed my concerns privately with Swaran Lata. She gave me her usual levelheaded advice. The shop next door had been vacant and I approached the owner. He was delighted as he had bought the shop to lease for rent collection and was saved the trouble of hunting for a suitable tenant. After necessary modifications to the newly acquired space, from two hundred square feet the shop now had an area of four hundred and ten square feet, more than double. The stationary counter would remain but greater emphasis would be given to the sale of books.

The shop was doing better than ever and it was with a tremendous sense of achievement that I began to contribute Rs. 5 to household expenses which rapidly rose to Rs. 10. In those days, five rupees was a good amount to live on comfortably. Of course, we had to watch our expenses but basic needs were covered and we could now afford the odd little luxury; we bought a little blue and white Lambretta scooter.

Life at the shop was not the only thing that was moving in the fast lane. At home, we were expecting our second child. Tanuj was born in August 1960. Her arrival was an auspicious event in our lives; with every smile she showered her blessings on our home and work alike. Life was getting better; the family lived well, dressed in good clothes and now there was enough to put by as savings.

Overall our pattern of spending remained much the same. The house was still running on Saubhagya's salary and any extra earnings were going into the bank for a rainy day or being used for the betterment of the shop. The kids were still small but they would grow up one day and would need funds for their future. So, little by little, we saved for their education and adulthood. Unaware of the years flashing past, in November 1962 our third child – a son – was born and the family was complete.

18

We were to spend twelve years in the house at Netaji Nagar. Our three children spent their early childhood surrounded by goodwill and caring neighbours. The residents of the colony began as strangers bound together through the necessity of carving out lives and earning a living. Hindus, Muslims, Punjabis, South Indians, high caste, low caste, dark, fair, refugees, non refugees: we all stood together and looked out for one another. The colony was the children's world and they grew up surrounded by an atmosphere of concern and affection and human warmth.

I was spending nearly ten hours at work everyday and would usually return home late in the night. This kept me away from my wife and children throughout the week. Saubhagya too, worked full time. It was during this period in our lives that we fully realized how blessed we were to have Swaran Lata as a friend. She loved the children as if they were her own and spent her free time caring for them. She taught at a Government school for girls in the Old City yet everyday she would make the twenty kilometre journey to Netaji Nagar so that she would be waiting for the children when they got home from school. She did her best to ensure that Neeraj, Tanuj and Anuj did not feel the absence of their parents. While Saubhagya and I worked hard at our respective jobs, Swaran Lata stood firm behind us, helping to guide our children through life. We may have thought twice before sending the children to stay with relatives but we were always happy for Swaran Lata to take them anywhere for days together. Many of the children's most memorable holidays were spent with her. She was a light and a guiding force in their lives and though she is no more, her memory remains with the family.

19

It was 1967 and we had saved nearly enough to be able to afford a house of our own. We had been very happy in the government colony, home for the past twelve years, but the three children were growing up. Although a little beyond our present means, we had enrolled them in the best schools. I wanted Saubhagya to leave her job and spend more time with the children at home. So in the same year we bought our first car, were allotted some land and began building our dream house.

Television was becoming popular and the sale of books suffered as a result. The money put aside for building our house did not stretch as far as we hoped but we managed to struggle on until the house was complete. A year later, after many months of personal supervision and the dedicated efforts of the architect, the house was finally built.

The enterprise had used up all our resources and we were left with very little to fall back on. The newly built house was ready for occupation but we could not afford to move in and call it home.

Another of my guardian angels, in the form of a Swiss journalist, provided the answer. Within a month of having finishing the construction, I met Peter Hess, who had moved to Delhi on an assignment. We met at the shop, found we thought alike on many subjects and became friends. Peter was tired of staying at a hotel and was looking for a place to rent. I offered him my newly constructed house. Peter loved it and decided to rent it for the princely amount Rs. 800 per month. This helped us replenish our diminished resources and to save money to decorate the house for the day when we would be able to move in ourselves.

Peter stayed with us for three more years. He was the first customer to change status from client to friend.

At last, in 1971, we moved into our own home.

I could now afford to run the house on my own income, my wife gave up her job and life took a turn for the better. We lived modestly but for the first time did not feel the pinch of money worries; there was that little extra for luxuries. We were happy, thought of the past and looked to a better future.

20

Throughout my life I have received tremendous, and often unexpected, support from others and it is to them I give credit for my success. Perhaps, as fellow refugees who experienced and understood hardship and realised the difference one kind soul or helping hand can make, my community was always ready to offer help. I spent my early adulthood in an atmosphere of support, care and concern and have always tried to extend this same warmth and goodwill and willingness to help to my customers.

Furthermore, I am grateful to my customers - to their patience and understanding. Because of them, I grew into the person I am today. I credit them with my learning and success.

I have always tried to be honest and fair and believe that hard work and a sincere approach will be recognised and, sooner or later, rewarded. Rather than hasty profits, I have followed a policy of reasonable and fair pricing that, over time, would be appreciated by my customers and gain their trust and loyalty. I made it a point to moderate my prices and my customer base grew.

Fulfillment has come through helping people; through listening to them and understanding their needs. It is rewarding to be able to anticipate your customer's wants and to be able to meet them. It is satisfying to know, after years of uncertainty, I can now gauge the prevailing trends and the tastes of regular and valued clients and can provide for these in advance.

In the beginning, I had no knowledge of my own. Customer's tastes and reading became my guide. In those days the selection of titles for the shop was based on direct requests. With encouragement from my patrons I became bolder in my selections. Treading on unfamiliar ground and taking small steps at first, I began increasing my choice of subjects. As a result, I think the shop now provides a unique range of books.

With experience came knowledge of the biggest names in publishing and I read catalogues tirelessly; devouring the entire booklists of all the big publishers on the first day that I received them. These lists became my lifeline. I would mark the titles of my choice on the lists and place the orders within days. Slowly, my confidence grew in my ability to gauge my customers' tastes. It was gratifying to see the books I had ordered moving off the shelves and to realise I was beginning to understand my clients.

Somehow, perhaps because my early customers were from the government world, the emphasis of my orders and stock is on current affairs, particularly politics, and international relations became a forte of the shop. I personally enjoy reading and selecting books on this topic. With Delhi being the capital city, the centre for rule and administration, there are many takers for this area of interest. The shop has always had a strong academic bias and the bookshelves have become a draw for the educated and intellectual elite of Delhi.

Many customers are 'known' faces; politicians and 'page three' people. Most of these visitors have praised the shop's diverse and unique collection of books and endorsed this by repeating their visits.

Khan Market is well situated to attract clients from the political world and civil service due to its position in the heart of the government residential areas. Khan Market is also close to the diplomatic enclave. Word soon spread of the shop's comprehensive collection of political and economic titles and attracted the working diplomatic community. Through word of mouth, the regular and loyal customer base has grown and the shop has settled into something of an institution of which I am proud. Those in the know have become regular visitors and have built a relationship with us.

The days became more tiring for me but, always ready to move on, breaking new ground has made me happy.

21

At first I did not know or recognise many of the people who frequented the shop but was content that my days were becoming busier.

The character of a person, city, area or even a shop depends on many things, not all of them tangible; the location of the shop turned out to be ideal: the stock grew to meet the needs of the general public and our niche clientele: I tried to provide a congenial atmosphere and good service and, most importantly, the freedom to browse. These factors combined to draw people back again and again and to build up a loyal clientelle. The appeal of the shop began to circulate by word of mouth and somehow, apart from its primary function as bookshop, it became a gathering place, particularly for the elite and literary world. Meetings that had not been concluded in the boardroom would be carried over to the shop.

The clients came from all walks of life; the newly appointed *babu**, the seasoned diplomat, the struggling engineer or doctor and the rich industrialist's playboy son. Customers who came into the shop as young Supreme Court advocates or bureaucrats on their first posting spent hours after work making their selections. As the shops reputation grew, the customers became Presidents, Prime Ministers, Chief Ministers, Ambassadors and other senior Diplomats. One evening the shop was honoured by a memorable visit from Late Vice President Shri Hidayatullah who complained to me about his hectic schedule which left him with no time to do the things he cherished and "can you imagine, people have now started selecting books for me. But I have not been here for so long so I have come to see some - on my own".

---

* Bureaucrat in the Indian Administrative Service

But all who enter the premises share a common desire, the search for knowledge and for something good to read. Knowing that books are expensive and to many a luxury and a habit not easily broken, I understand the joy of browsing. The premises are small and usually crowded but everyone is allowed to continue looking. Most of the customers have limited resources and in their place I would probably do the same.

Schoolchildren would come in, sit in a corner and read until the evening. Occasionally, one would slip a comic in to his bag and walk out. Often, they had an idea that I had seen them but had remained quiet and they carried this guilt for many years. Boys, now grown into men, have come to me ten, fifteen and even twenty years later and sheepishly apologised for their misdemeanor. Some of these boys are now in important positions, educated and representing the country. I feel proud of them - that they were able to come back and admit to their small dishonesty and to apologise.

There have been years and even generations of association with customers and some clients became lifelong friends. Customers came to the shop as little children and have continued to do so over the past fifty years. I think it is these relationships that are the cornerstone of the shops success, through which it has achieved its name and the respect of its clientele.

22

The years rolled by and the shop took on its distinct identity. We were attracting dignitaries from the world over. The creation of extra floor space by taking over the adjacent two shops meant a further boon to booklovers - more room to browse.

Anuj, my son, was now a teenager and after school he began spending an hour or two helping me in the shop. He enjoyed working with books and had a sharp memory for titles. But most of all liked to talk to the customers and spent most of his free time on the shop floor.

In 1980 Anuj began University and had more free time and would spend half the day working at the shop.

This gave me more time to spend compiling the information we send out to customers. Surprisingly, Anuj and I have the same interests when it comes to selecting books for the shop; security studies and international relations, politics and economics.

Not shy, Anuj was comfortable chatting to strangers which helped to maintain goodwill. He would - without inhibition - mingle with the clients and discuss their needs. He liked to understand the books that he sold and more importantly, he liked to understand the customers' tastes. Each new topic presented another world to him and he appreciated the aspect of his profession that allowed him to easily pursue a subject so deeply. Together we began to explore new topics to display on the shelves and I think we make a good team.

The shop now acts as a meeting ground for intellectual gatherings. People stay in the shop for hours selecting their books and wrap up meetings carried over from work. The shop offers them an ambience of intellect and casualness that a tired mind comes looking for and we even serve coffee!

Customers feel at ease in the shop and spontaneously enjoy debating on topics that they would not discuss at formal gatherings. Some even schedule 'after hours' meetings at the premises. It is common to pick up snatches of conversation on parliament or the happenings in the political arena. Often, while helping the customers to select their books, Anuj joins in. This helped him considerably in reaching his decisions to add a small publishing division to the store.

While listening to customers he looks for any gaps in material available on various topics and mentally takes note to fill in those gaps. He does independent research until he is able to find the most informative book on the subject, sometimes several books. Customers find this gesture extremely helpful and time and again come back with requests they are having trouble with. We both attend meetings and conventions to help us keep up to date with the changing trends and demands of the reading world. We are interested in anything that keeps our scholarly clients' minds stimulated and do everything we can to help them acquire the information they need.

Now I am less active as my son has taken over the day-to-day affairs of the shop. What began as a means of support for a young man struggling to provide for his family has grown into something of an institution in the book world. Although I have always been motivated by work rather than its fruits, I nonetheless look back with satisfaction on a fulfilling career and one that I may well have chosen if the choice had been open to me. The journey started fifty years ago has finally been rewarded with the goodwill and trust of loyal customers. Today at 75 I am proud to be associated with the learned and the intellectuals of society…. proud to be the vendor of knowledge, proud to be a bookseller.

Relationships

*P*erhaps the one thing that stands out when I look back is that the joy in my life and the success of my shop has depended on relationships. I have been touched and pleased to read the felicitations and stories sent in by my patrons and friends whose faces are almost as familiar as those of my own family. I thought it would be interesting to read what this relationship has meant to them, in their own words. Below are their writings............

As a young teenager interested in books, your father, while meticulous with his small change was equally generous with the credit he extended. These periods must have often tested his patience. He has always stretched himself and his team to find that elusive book I have often felt I could not live without.

It was once far less crowded and busy where you could spend hours. It was a reassuring space just to be in, not always to buy books I knew I could not afford. I remember being awed by the presence of the 'whose who' of the literati who used to and continue to frequent the shop. It has retained its warm welcoming ambiance and the womb like intellectual reassurance embedded in the world of books, its staff and your father's affection, not to mention your more youthful exuberance in recent years. I was delighted and blessed to have your father attend the recent launch of my first book by His Holiness The Dalai Lama and to see it on sale at your shop. It sort of completed a cycle. Bahri Sons has remained virtually a place of pilgrimage each time I am in the vicinity.

Rajiv Mehrotra
Foundation for Universal Responsibility

I built a house in Golf Links almost 50 years ago, when the dense forest cover extended into Golf Links and jackals would prowl into the stillness of night, and over the years have seen my children and then grand children grow (as also this metropolis of Delhi) and the blossoming and development of the refugees of partition's market i.e. Khan Market, one particular shop - Bahri & Sons - has stood out as hallmark of this rapidly changing yet constant horizon.

Dr. Jugal Kishore

A ladder which everyone should try to climb. Bahri's have been an institution cultivating knowledge... and should remain always such with our goodwill & affection.

R. K. Mehra
Rupa & Co.

The courtesy and consideration shown by Bahri Sahab at all times which has endeared him to us, so that we do not regard ourselves as his customers but as his family members. I have on numerous occasions visited Waterstones and W.H.Smith in London and even there I said to myself, "There is no shop quite like Bahri Sons".

As a young child at school I was in awe of Bahri

Sahab - and even now, I am still overawed by him... Bahri Sahab made me buy "The World of Physics" for my son, Amarendra, when he was 13 years old. That kindled in him a great love for physics and today he is doing his doctorate in the subject at Imperial College, London. Bahri Sons has played a key role in our lives and that of our children.

Mrs. Krishna Swarup
Advocate

When I first entered Bahrisons I did not expect to experience a pang of nostalgia - my father once owned a successful bookshop in Lahore and I felt that his shop must have been very like this. And Mr Bahri reminded me of my father, with his old world courtesy and concern for the customer.

My father, too, was forced to abandon his home during the partition and he lost his beloved bookshop. But the expression that 'destination is not destiny' is perhaps apt here. My father somehow was never able to turn the clock back and begin again whereas Mr Bahri is now the proprietor of not just a shop, but also a successful institution in the world of books.

I have visited the shop for over 20 years now and my daughter bought her first book there. For me, Bahrisons feels, not like a bookshop, but a library. You can pick up the books, read the extracts of your choice, return them to the shelf - you are free to browse to your heart's content.

Small and cosy, you will not find the indifference of the commercial bookshop here. You can get into lively discussions with father and son and may even be offered a cup of coffee. The Bahris are genuine and sincere people.

Books are your best friends, they accept you as you are, don't criticise you and can be your constant companions - books mean a lot to me.

When I am overstretched and need re-charging, I head down to Khan Market and Bahrisons and browse, pick up books and drift into another world and soon I feel my spirits lift and I am my old self again.

D.K.Berry, Vice President
Taj Hotels & Resorts, New Delhi

Mr. Balraj Bahri, the epitome of courtesy and old world charm, has not only seen me grow up but also my wife and her family, who too were regulars at his shop. The association and friendship is therefore two-fold, in fact three, for most of our daughter's books have also come from Bahri Sons.

We have seen the bookshop grow from its modest beginnings to what it is today, perhaps the most comprehensively stocked bookshop in Delhi. Its eclectic collection of books caters to the widest range of customers some of whom demand esoteric titles not easily available elsewhere. Bahri Sons seem to have it all, for all ages and tastes. It is a pleasure to browse in this shop, the time effortlessly slipping away.

Anuj Bahri, who now runs the bookshop, and its publishing wing, is a mine of information, deeply interested in his profession. He is assisted by a helpful and courteous staff, always willing to rummage through the shelves to locate whichever book is desired, while you wait sipping a cold drink or coffee.

In retirement as well I spend many happy hours at Bahri Sons ... and chatting to father and son, even if

I am no longer able to buy as many books as I would like to, for I find that this itself is an education.

Dalip Mehta
Indian Foreign Service (retired)

I have used the excellent services of Bahrisons for India International Centre Library from time to time during the last 36 years and have always come across a rich variety of publications at Bahri Sons.

H K Kaul
Chief Librarian, India International Centre

Like many other Punjabi families who experienced the traumas of communal riots and the partition of 1947, landing up in Delhi as homeless refugees, Mr. Bahri ...showed his inner strength and courage to start life anew and began to run a Bookshop.

I do not know what was the motivation behind his decision to run a Bookshop, except as is written in his book - "sheer survival". But whatever the vision he had at that time, I wonder if he ever imagined that his shop would not only continue for 50 years but would develop into one of the most popular and sought after shops in town.

Going down the corridors of time I remember how in the late fifties, my late father-in-law, Mr. Gowardhandas veteran freedom fighter of Punjab was always keen to read any new book written on the new China, on Non-alignment and such political and social topics of the day, and my late husband, Shri Yudister Kumar, Barrister at Law would invariably bring them home from Bahri's along with ones of his choice.

What has been the reason for its success? Obviously the wholehearted dedication of the founder to satisfy each of his readers in providing him the books of his choice. From such a huge number of books, it always seemed so easy for Mr. Bahri to find the one that was asked for, and if not, it would be sent for and made available in record time... and tradition has survived the passing years.

Mrs Jyoti Bose, my daughter and Principal of Springdales School, Dhaula Kuan - an avid reader, swears by Bahri's.

"If you can't get this book in Bahris, she says, then you can't get it anywhere"!

Bahri's personalized friendly atmosphere has been the hallmark of its success.

Rajni Kumar (Mrs)
Chairperson, Springdales Education Society

The huge signboard, on entry into Khan Market, is almost a welcome arch ..

Mr. Bahri .....the way he presides over his enterprise has that air of quiet dignity that fits well with the ambience. And it has more to it than the mere presence of his generously groomed military whiskers! Adversity, and deprivation faced at partition, have given him the resilience, and will to succeed - without the bitterness that accompanies similar circumstances. And that spirit rubs off on the enormous clientele he has attracted over the years.

Om Arora
The Variety Book Depot, New Delhi

We salute a great man of immense simplicity and vision - a man who gave both direction and sense of pride to the community as a whole and the world of books, in particular. In so doing we also salute the great institution he built... and nurtured.

Harkin D Chatlani
India Book Distributors, Mumbai.

Courage, determination and honesty are the pillars on which your father has built Bahri Sons as a landmark in Khan Market.

Renu Modi
Gallery Espace, New Delhi

I am not quite sure why I stop in Khan Market every time I pass that way. This, despite living five minutes away for fifty years. Old habits die hard. Khan Market is not what it used to be. It is not with little regret and sadness that I walk before the crowded shops of this now most fashionable area wishing for things to be the way they were – quiet stores with smiling keepers, each with a smile and a nod of recognition.

I think it would be fair to say that not all is lost and that bahrisons must not, like many a good book be judged by its cover. Quite frankly, they did not need that big yellow big sign. *The store served the community well* and continues to draw hordes of booklovers everyday. *The bookstore remains as it was: helpful, smiling staff ready at hand, unlimited by an obvious by a space constraint, a neatly arranged, wide range of titles and an enviable talent of having heard of and locating almost any title you throw at them, digging out books from impossible places in a matter of minutes.*

Started in 1953, I think what sets this store apart from the others is that - the store is quite possibly the Life of Mr. Bahri and his son.

V K Madhavan Kutty., Padma Shree
Journalist